Fun Mummy

By **Steve Bertman**

Illustrated by **Ethan Long**

STERLING

New York / London
www.sterlingpublishing.com/kids

For Andrew, Josh, Jordyn, Logan, and Brandon
—S.B.

To Mary, my Step Mummy and friend.
—E.L.

STERLING and the distinctive Sterling logo are registered trademarks of
Sterling Publishing Co., Inc.

Library of Congress Cataloging-in-Publication Data
Bertman, Steve.
  Funny mummy / by Steve Bertman ; illustrated by Ethan Long.
     p. cm.
  Includes bibliographical references.
  ISBN 978-1-4027-6910-8
  1. Mummies–Juvenile humor. 2. Wit and humor, Juvenile. I. Long, Ethan, ill. II. Title.
  PN6231.M79B47 2010
  818'.602–dc22

                          2009052676

Lot#: 10 9 8 7 6 5 4 3 2 1
05/10

Published by Sterling Publishing Co., Inc.
387 Park Avenue South, New York, NY 10016
Text © 2010 by Steve Bertman
Illustrations © 2010 by Ethan Long
Distributed in Canada by Sterling Publishing
c/o Canadian Manda Group, 165 Dufferin Street
Toronto, Ontario, Canada M6K 3H6
Distributed in the United Kingdom by GMC Distribution Services
Castle Place, 166 High Street, Lewes, East Sussex, England BN7 1XU
Distributed in Australia by Capricorn Link (Australia) Pty. Ltd.
P.O. Box 704, Windsor, NSW 2756, Australia

Sterling ISBN 978-1-4027-6910-8

For information about custom editions, special sales, premium and
corporate purchases, please contact Sterling Special Sales
Department at 800-805-5489 or specialsales@sterlingpublishing.com.

CONTENTS

Introduction   5

Jokes and Riddles   6

Glossary   92

Some Children's Books about
    Ancient Egypt   94

About the Author   96

INTRODUCTION

The smile on King Tut's golden mask has puzzled experts for generations. What could explain it? The Egyptian scrolls preserved in museums certainly don't contain any chuckles.

One explorer was determined to unravel the mystery. For half a century he searched the shifting sands of Egypt, wearing out camel after camel, until finally he found a buried tomb filled with dust, and under the dust was an amazing treasure: an ancient best seller written in hilarious hieroglyphics.

Today, thanks to his sensational discovery, you, too, can read the oldest ridiculous book in the world: *Funny Mummy*, the book that made dried-out pharaohs like Tut crack up.

If you're looking for laughs, read on and learn the pyramid-age punch lines to such eternal questions as:

What did Cleopatra's doctor tell her?

How did the mummy become a movie actor?

Why were Egyptian bicycles so hard to ride?

If, mortal one, you desire to know over 350 one-liners on such ageless topics as sports, school, entertainment, family, food, and health, then turn this fateful page.

JOKES and RIDDLES

Why did the cook pour tomato sauce over the royal mummy's chest?

The pharaoh had ordered barbequed ribs.

How do you get out of a tomb?

Just climb up the *scares*.

If a mummy is vertical when he's standing, what is he when he's lying down?

*Horror*zontal.

How did the mummy get into show business?

They put his leg in the cast.

What do you call a pyramid built in France?

A *Pierre*amid.

What did the Italian archaeologist say when he opened the sarcophagus?

"*Mummy* mia!"

How do you join a party on the Nile?

Just barge in.

How do mummies correspond?

By *eek*-mail.

What did the computer-expert mummy call his wrappings?

Softwear.

How does a mummy feel when you bother him in his tomb?

Ag-*grave*-ated.

Whom did the pharaoh blame when things weren't described right?

De scribe.

What was the Hungarian mummy's favorite dish?

*Ghoul*ash.

How did a mummy feel after eating?

Crumby.

Why did the mummy have bad luck bowling?

His thumb stayed in the ball.

Sister: Why do those palm trees seem
far off, brother?
Brother: Because they're o-asis.

What was wrong with the low glyphics?

They should have been *hier*.

What do you call a round-trip to a tomb?

A re-*hearse*-al.

Why were mummies so brave?

They kept a stiff upper lip.

Where did they bury the pharaoh's cat?

In a *purr*amid.

How ugly was King Cheops?

He had a face only a *mummy* could love.

What was ancient Egypt's favorite drink?

Diet soda.

What did the mummy say when he got a phone call?

"I can't talk now. I'm all tied up."

Why can you always count on a mummy for help?

He can always lend you a hand.

What was a kid mummy's favorite doll?

Raggedy Ann.

What did the mummy lawyer say at the end of the trial?

"I rest my case."

What newspaper did mummies read?

The Daily Gauzette

What did King Tut's lawyer read after Tut died?

His last will and *tut*sament.

Why was the mummy convict angry?

He got a bum wrap.

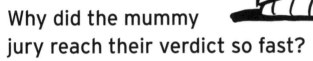

Why did the mummy jury reach their verdict so fast?

It was an open and shut case.

How do mummies know what's going to happen tomorrow?

They read their *horror*scopes.

Why did the ambitious archaeologist reach into the sarcophagus?

He wanted to get *a head*.

Where did mummies like to go for vacation?

Tombstone, Arizona.

How did the mummy dress for her birthday party?

She came gift-wrapped.

Why was the mummy worried when they buried him in a cucumber?

He was in a real pickle.

How far in Egypt did news travel?

From *ghost* to *ghost*.

Why was the mummy worried?

He was in a real bind.

Why was the mummy fired?

He was lying down on the job.

Why did the archaeologist take a calculator along on his trip?

To find out how *mummy* were in the tomb.

Why did the post office put a stamp on the pharaoh's face?

He was classified "mummy, male."

What mummy housecleaning job took the most time?

Dusting.

What did mummies study in college?

*Eek*ology.

What was the mummy's summer like?

*Balm*y.

Why did the mummy wear glasses?

He wanted to *reed*.

Why did the embarrassed mummy insist on having his head bandaged?

He didn't want to lose face.

Why did the mummy go for a swim?

He wanted to *ghoul* off.

Why did the mummy enjoy being taken out of his coffin?

It gave him a lift.

Why did the mummy dislike fighting?

He had no stomach for it.

Why was it so hard to find honest musicians in ancient Egypt?

Because there was a *lyre* in every band.

Why didn't the pharaoh pay attention to the workmen singing in the quarry?

They were just another rock group.

How do you know if a mummy orchestra knows the latest tunes?

Just check the *band age*.

**What did the mummy
do when he got excited?**

He simply lost his head.

**What kind of hamburger
did a mummy order at
a restaurant?**

A Thebes-burger.

**What song do French mummies
always sing?**

"Pharaoh Jacques."

**What was the weather forecast in
Cairo, Egypt?**

Cloudy and *ghoul*.

What kind of door leads to a tomb?

A *scream* door.

How did the pharaoh's dog find him?

She was digging for old bones.

What did the mummy say to the garbage collector?

"Something *Sphinx* around here."

What were Egyptian ambulance drivers called?

Pyramedics.

After being caught, what did one grave-robber say to the other?

"I'm not going to take the wrap for this alone."

How did the pharaoh cross the Nile?

On a *pharr*y.

What were bobby socks called in Egypt?

*Ankh*lets.

How did the mummy become a movie actor?

He passed his Hollywood *scream* test.

Why did the owner of the mummy nightclub fire his new comic?

Because when the audience heard his jokes, they cracked up.

How do you buy a mummy?

Put it on layaway.

What are souvenirs of old pharaohs called?

*Mumm*entos.

Which mummy brothers invented the airplane?

The *Fright* Brothers.

What did the newspaper editor think of the mummy's biography?

Obit long.

What do you call an Egyptian tale with a suspenseful ending?

A *glyph*-hanger.

Do mummy musicians die?

No. They just de-compose.

What kind of music did mummies like best?

Ragtime.

Why can you never believe what a mummy says?

Because he is always *lie*ing in his coffin.

Which letters did mummies fear most?

D, K.

How do you know when a mummy is an adult?

When he is all *groan*.

What kind of invitation did mummies send?

An engraved one.

Why did the pharaoh always hit the bull's-eye?

He was a dead shot.

Why wasn't there room in the tomb for the pharaoh's dentist?

There were no more cavities.

What did Mummyville Elementary have a lot of?

School spirits.

What do you call it when you go crazy in the desert?

Insandity.

What did mummies do on Monday nights?

Watched *Mummy Night Football.*

What did the sign say in the window of the Egyptian funeral parlor?

"Satisfaction guaranteed or your *mummy* back."

What magic words did Egyptian magicians say?

"Have-a-cadaver."

Why did they think the mummy was self-centered?

He was all wrapped up in himself.

Why did Mark Antony say Italy was like perfume?

It had a *nice-a Roma*.

What did mummies eat for Thanksgiving?

Turkey, *grave*-y, and cran*bury* sauce.

Why did the pharaoh put whipped cream on his pyramid?

It was his favorite *desert* topping.

How do you measure a smelly mummy?

In *scent*imeters.

What were mummy recipes called?

Soul food.

What was the mummy's favorite Mexican dish?

Hot *tomb*-ales.

What did the lady mummy wear to the party?

A pair of *Nile*-ons.

What birthday present do you buy for a mummy with cold hands?

A warm *pyramid*-ens.

What was ancient Egypt's favorite game show?

Name That Tomb!

Why did the pharaoh take an elephant along on his trip?

He thought he might need an extra trunk.

What happened to the mummy who auditioned for TV?

They couldn't put him on live, so they taped him.

What was the mummy's favorite dessert?

Isis cream.

What did the mummy anchorman say at the end of the news?

"Well, that wraps it up for today."

What did mummies like to watch on TV on Saturday mornings?

Car*tombs*.

What did polite mummies do before they ate?

They washed their hands in the *Sphinx*.

What was the mummy's favorite vegetable?

Tomb-atoes.

Who made Egyptian cheesecake?

Sahara Lee.

What was the name of the ancient Egyptian who put cans of spinach in his tomb?

Popeye-*rus*.

What's the best part about staying at a mummy hotel?

Tomb service.

What was the mummy's favorite picnic lunch?

*Sand*wiches.

What was the final score in the mummy football game?

It was all tied up.

What was the mummy team's favorite cheer?

"Ra! Ra! Ra!"

Why did the mummies play baseball in the tomb?

They had plenty of bats.

What did the golf pro tell the mummy?

"Stay on the *pharaoh*-way and watch out for that big sand trap!"

How did a mummy golfer exit a pyramid?

He made a hole in one.

What did the workers say when they finished building the pyramid?

"It's all *dune*."

If you need a glyphic to finish your inscription, what do you do?

You *hier a glyphic*.

What do you call a look-alike mummy?

A dead ringer.

What kind of doctor did the mummy go to when he hurt his back?

A *Cairo*-practor.

How did the doctor know the mummy was sick?

He was *coffin* a lot.

What did the doctor tell Cleopatra over the phone?

"Just take two *asps* and call me in the morning."

What was ancient Egypt's favorite card game?

Gin *mummy*.

Why didn't the near-sighted pharaoh finish building his pyramid?

He couldn't see the point.

What kind of operation did the pharaoh have?

A *tut*silectomy.

What did the archaeologist say when he found his second aluminum mummy?

"Foiled again!"

If you ordered a whole sarcophagus but only got half a sarcophagus, what did the salesman do?

Egypt you.

Why did they embalm the frog?

He croaked.

Who finished the pyramid when the workers went on strike?

A skeleton crew.

Why was the mummy a coward?

He didn't have any guts.

How did the ancient Egyptian wind up with fifteen fingers?

He asked a friend to lend him a hand.

What did the mummy say when he heard a stupid joke?

"It *Sphinx*."

What was ancient history's least tidy country?

*Messy*potamia.

Who climbed down chimneys in Egypt and left gifts for children?

Sandy Claus.

What happened when the mummy ate too much?

She got a *tomb*-y ache.

How did the tomb robber get caught?

He made a grave mistake.

Why was the mummy-embalming business so hard?

There was stiff competition.

How attractive was the female mummy?

Too *boo*-tiful for words.

When does Cleopatra turn on the charm?

When Julius *Caesar*.

Who did the mummy get to write her biography?

A ghostwriter.

How did the mummy lose all her wrappings?

She got caught in a *tore*-nado.

What were Egyptian kids good at in math?

*Mummify*ing and dividing.

In Egypt, if you missed the old bus, what could you always count on?

Anubis.

When the fleeing tomb-robber saw his getaway chariot had a flat tire, what did he do?

He turned to *de spare*.

Where did a mummy fill up his tank?

At *aghast* station.

Why didn't the mummy tell her best friend the truth?

She didn't have the heart.

What did the mummies say when they dined at a French restaurant?

"*Bone* appetit!"

Why couldn't the mummy keep driving his chariot?

He was on a dead-end street.

What does a mummy do at the end of a hard day?

He unwinds.

Why was the Egyptian stand-up comic a hit?

He kept his audience in stitches.

What personal quality was most admired in ancient Egypt?

*Dead*ication.

What did "R.I.P." stand for on an Egyptian tomb?

"Rest in pieces."

What kept the mummy from falling apart?

Crazy glue.

Why was the pharaoh only twelve inches tall?

He was just an average ruler.

Why did mummies avoid health foods?

There weren't enough preservatives.

What was Egypt's most awful breakfast cereal?

Dreaded Wheat.

What did the mummies call Napoleon?

*Bone*aparte.

Why did they call the moldy mummy an environmentalist?

He turned green.

How is building a pyramid like playing baseball?

You first need to get men on base.

How did Egyptians take their morning coffee?

De*coffin*ated.

What was the mummy's favorite hairstyle?

*Dread*locks.

Why were old mummy wrappings valued?

They were thought to be *hole-y.*

What do you call the inside of a tomb?

Forbidden *terror*tory.

What style of writing did they teach in mummy school?

Curse-ive.

How do you know mummies have a sense of humor?

They can always crack a smile.

What egg dish did mummies like to eat for breakfast?

A ham and cheese *amulet*.

Who wrote bedtime stories for little mummies?

The Brothers *Grim*.

How did the Copts of Egypt get around?

By helicopter.

What do you call an embalmed yellow bird?

A scary canary.

What was the mummy's favorite fall holiday?

Holloween.

**Mummy No. 1: "Are you absolutely sure?"
Mummy No. 2: "Of *corpse* I am!"**

What did ancient Egyptians call five babies born at the same time?

Quin*tut*lets.

What was an Egyptian mummy's favorite pizza topping?

Papyroni.

What toy did mummy kids like best?

A *ghoula*-hoop.

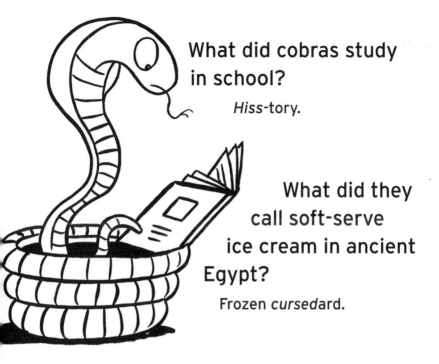

What did cobras study in school?

Hiss-tory.

What did they call soft-serve ice cream in ancient Egypt?

Frozen *cursed*ard.

Why did mummies like to shop at discount malls?

So they could *haunt* for bargains.

What was the mummy's blood type?

*AB*sent.

What did people call the pharaoh who offered them a ride?

A *chariot*able fellow.

When a mummy lost one of his eyeballs in public, what did he do?

He hired a private eye.

What did mummies put on their breakfast cereal?

Buries.

Why aren't wet mummies any fun?

They're damp rags.

Who was the grittiest military commander ever to rule Egypt?

Alex*sand*er the Great.

Where did the mommy and daddy mummy lay their baby down for her nap?

In her *crypt*.

How did mummies sign their letters?

"*Bury* truly yours."

How was the mummy talent show?

Simply *spook*tacular!

How did mummies manage to eat a balanced diet?

They studied the food pyramid.

What did one Egyptian sweetheart say to the other?

"I'm simply en*wrap*tured with you!"

When a mummy was annoyed at something, what did he do?

He made no bones about it.

In Egypt, what did builders put on top of pyramids in case of a thunderstorm?

*Frighten*ing rods.

What's the hardest part about making a mummy's bed?

Changing the *shrieks*.

Why do mummies make good spies?

They're always undercover.

Why did the mummy go shopping?

She needed some new threads.

What did Mark Antony want to know before he bought his sweetheart a cat?

When would *Cleo pet her*?

Why is exploring a dark tomb like taking part in the Olympics?

You have to pass the torch.

Why was the mummy late for dinner?

He got all wrapped up in his work.

What kind of sandwich did they find buried next to the old mummy?

Peanut butter and *smelly*.

What kind of music did Egyptian builders listen to when they moved pyramid blocks?

Rock and roll.

What did the doctor tell the mummy parents after their son's annual physical?

"He *grue*-some."

What did you find in the pantry of every tomb?

*Gross*eries.

When a mummy got sick to his stomach, what did he have?

A *phantom*my ache.

How expensive was the mummy's funeral?

It cost him an arm and a leg.

How did the mummy help his buddy who was looking for a job?

He pulled some strings for him.

What did the mummy say to her sweetheart?

"I'm glad we wound up together."

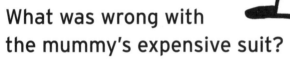

What did the lookout say to the tomb robber?

"The ghost is clear!"

What was wrong with the mummy's expensive suit?

It was a rip-off.

Why did the pharaoh's coffin float when it fell into the Nile?

You can lead a *hearse* to water but you can't make it *sink*.

How did the race inside the pyramid end?

Dead even.

What was on the menu at all mummy restaurants?

Knuckle sandwiches.

What did mummies call an easy math problem?

A no-brainer.

What do you call a friendly Egyptian corpse?

A chummy mummy.

How thorough were the tomb robbers?

They left no stone unturned.

What kind of artist was the mummy?

A *skull*pter.

What did the Egyptian priests say when their sacred scrolls caught on fire?

"Holy smoke!"

Why did the mummified pharaoh stop listening to his advisors?

They talked his ear off.

How did the tomb builder call the mummy meeting to order?

By pounding his *gravel*.

How did mummies make their smiles so scary?

When they brushed, they used tooth-*fright*ener.

How could the doctor tell the mummy had a sore throat?

When he talked, he was really *Horus*.

What was ancient Egypt's favorite candy?

Chocolate-covered *Amuns*.

What did the Egyptian scribe send his wife on her birthday?

A dozen red *Rosettas.*

Why did the tired scribe chase the alphabet?

He wanted to catch some Zs.

Why did they give the pharaoh a second funeral?

They wanted to re*hearse.*

Why was the pyramid builder so persistent?

He wanted to make his point.

How did the mummy husband increase his IQ?

His wife gave him a piece of her mind.

Why was the mummy so tiny?

She was shrink-wrapped.

What kept Egyptian dentists so busy?

Filling all those cavities.

Why was the mummy so undecided about staying?

He had half a mind to leave.

Where did the pharaoh go to get his prescription filled?

The *pharaoh*macy.

Why did the mummy think she had been embalmed wrong?

She just had a gut feeling.

Why did the policeman think the tomb robber had reformed?

Because he had turned over a new *thief*.

What did mummies order at a Mexican restaurant?

*Boo*ritos and re*fright* beans.

Why did the mummified cat run so slowly?

She would always *paws*.

What did the sympathetic mummy say?

"My heart goes out to you."

Why were Egyptian mummy maids busy all the time?

They were always turning to dust.

Why are mummy wrappings so good to eat?

They stick to your ribs.

What did mummies like best about Christmas?

Unwrapping all those present.

Where did the priestess of the cat goddess get her pet?

From a *cat*alogue.

What did Egyptian embalmers like to listen to?

Organ music.

What did the mummy do when his legs were lost at the mortuary?

He came back *short*ly.

What do you call a pharaoh who's always complaining?

A *moan*arch.

What did the mummy say when his sweetheart's tomb collapsed?

"I had a crush on you."

What did they find when they examined the body of the one hundred-year-old pharaoh?

A long liver.

What did King Cheops order for dinner?

Pork *Cheops*.

Where did ancient Egyptians go to check out scrolls?

The *lie-bury*.

What did mummies use when they were short on cash?

*Dread*it cards.

Why didn't the mummy climb to the very top of the pyramid?

He didn't have the stomach for it.

Where did mummies mail their letters?

At the *ghost* office.

What do you call the toothless mummy?

Gummy.

How did the forgetful mummy lose his memory?

He buried his head in the sand.

How did the mummy go broke?

He went from riches to rags.

Why did the camels return to the cabbage farmer?

It was the *slaw* that *brought* the camels back.

Where did they bury the queen who shopped till she dropped?

In a *mall*soleum.

What do you get when you butter and broil a piece of papyrus?

Filet of *scroll*.

What do you call a mummy who makes sure pyramids are built right?

A building in*spectre*.

What is a mixed-up embalming job called?

An *au*topsy-turvy.

Why did the angry mummy smell like perfume?

She was incensed.

What made the mummy department store go out of business?

Stiff competition.

What song did mummies sing as they sat around the campfire at night?

"*Tomb*-Ba-Yah."

What force keeps a corpse in its tomb?

Grave-ity.

Why is a grown-up mummy uglier than a child mummy?

Because it's more *growt*esque.

How do you measure the temperature of a scary tomb?

With a *terror*mometer.

How did the mummy feel about being in a dark tomb?

He was simply de-lighted.

What were kids called in Egypt?

Juve*Nile*s.

What did an ancient Egyptian always say when he ate his salad?

"*Olive* forever."

What did the talkative Mesopotamian mummy always do?

Babylon.

Why didn't mummies ever have to buy shoes?

Their *soles* were immortal.

How do you get a pharaoh to let you do what you want?

Ask his *pyramid*sion.

In ancient Egypt, what chores did mummy children do?

They straightened up their tombs and made up their sarcophaguses.

Why did the Egyptian priest like Swiss cheese?

He found its *hole*-iness appealing.

Where did the High Priest get headaches?

In his temples.

Why did the rabbit dig down to the pharaoh's tomb?

Someone told him the king's treasure was *24-carrot*.

When water birds were embalmed, what were they wrapped in?

Duck tape.

What happened to the thief when he got caught in the doorway of a tomb?

He found himself in a big *jamb*.

At dinner, how did Mrs. Tut feel when her husband praised her quiche?

She was simply *egg*static.

After being entombed for 5,000 years, how did the queen's perfume smell?

Vial.

In what part of his tomb did the mummy do his complaining?

The *whine* cellar.

What U.S. state loves mummy jokes the most?

Pun-silly-vania.

What was the name of a famous pirate mummy?

Long John *Shivers*.

Why did the well-wrapped mummy go far in life?

He was bound to succeed.

Why did the mummy cross the road?

To pick up a piece of himself he left on the other side.

Why were Egyptian bicycles hard to ride?

The wheels were carved out of stone.

Why did mummies eat seafood?

They thought it was bene*fish*al.

When the mummies got married, what did they vow?

To live together "for better or *hearse*."

Who are the scientists who unlock history's secrets?

Ar*key*ologists.

Where do archaeologists find the words to describe their discoveries?

In the *dig*tionary.

What did the disintegrating mummy say to the jokester?

"Don't pull my leg!"

What did the sign over the scribe's office door say?

"There's no business like *scroll* business."

What crime did the cat goddess commit when she lied on the stand?

*Purr*jury.

Why did it take the mummy pitcher so long to throw the ball?

He had to complete his windup.

What is Egypt's weather like when warm breezes blow?

*Emb*almy.

What did the grateful cobra say?

"Fang you very much!"

What did Supermummy stay away from?

The *crypt-at-night*.

What kind of tape did they put on King Tut's face?

*Mask*ing tape.

What's the motto of mummy cooperation?

"You *patch* my back and I'll *patch* yours."

Why was the tomb robber riding on the back of a little sheep?

He was on the *lamb*.

What kind of dessert do they sell at a mummy bake sale?

Boston *scream* pie.

Why did the bankrupt undertakers glue the two mummies together?

They were just trying to make ends meet.

What card game did the sun god Ra play by himself?

*Solar*taire.

What did the visitor to the tomb say when he inspected the bones?

"Say, what kind of joint is this?"

Where did the mummy find supplies to fix up his old tomb?

The local *tomb* improvement store.

What was the ancient Egyptian name for a fiddle?

A *die*olin.

When the mummy unwrapped himself starting at his toes, where did he end up?

At his wit's end.

Why did the pharaoh hire a bunch of potatoes to guard his tomb?

He figured they'd keep their eyes peeled.

How did mummies sing "The Battle Hymn of the Republic"?

"Gory, gory, hallelujah!"

Why didn't the mummy chef smile more?

It was simply his deadpan expression.

Why do mummies walk so slowly?

They can't step lively.

Why can mummies get away with lying?

They can keep a straight face.

Why did the mummy businessman climb out of his coffin?

He wanted to think outside the box.

What did the shoeless mummy feel when he lost the marathon?

The agony of *da feet*.

Why did the mummy dig a hole just inside the front entrance to the pyramid?

It was a tourist trap.

Who was ancient Egypt's most energetic pharaoh?

Pepi.

For what discovery did the pharaoh's chief scientist win the Nobel Prize?

He found a *pure* for the common *gold*.

When mummies play hockey, what's the easiest (and scariest) part?

The face-off.

What did they call it when they lowered the computer programmer's mummy into his tomb?

Downloading.

What kinds of tests did mummy teachers give?

Boo or false.

Why didn't pharaohs last very long on the throne?

Heir today. Gone tomorrow.

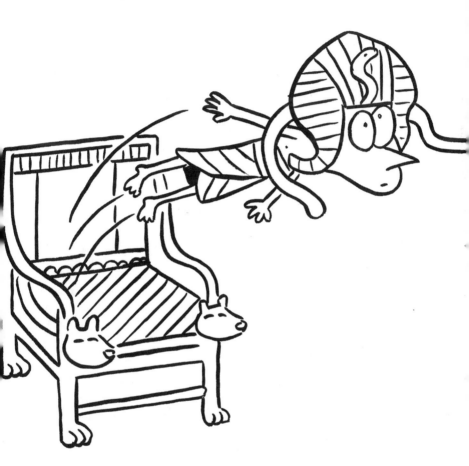

When the royal treasury was ransacked, why did they blame the pharaoh?

They figured it was his *vault*.

Who was the archaeologist's favorite English detective?

Sherlock *Bones.*

What did the mummy do when he eyed a bat?

He didn't bat an eye.

Why did the tap-dancing mummy carry a crowbar?

He wanted to break into show business.

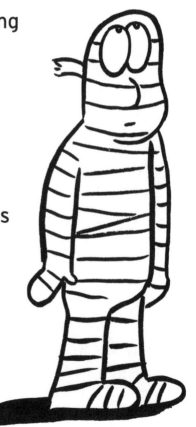

Where did mummies go to have fun on some really wicked rides?

A carne*vil.*

What was the pharaoh's favorite flower?

Chrysanthe*mummies*.

How beautiful was the mummified queen?

Drop-dead gorgeous.

In the Cairo Symphony Orchestra, what instrument did the skeleton play?

Trom*bone*.

What did the gravedigger say as the cement hardened?

"The plot thickens."

Why did the mummy asked to be double-wrapped?

He needed to sit tight.

In ancient Egypt, why did writing require so much work?

You had to put a *pyramid* at the end of every sentence.

What did mummy moms and their kids do every September?

Shopped for *ghoul* supplies.

Why were school kids in ancient Egypt always so tired?

They had to carry stone tablets around in their backpacks.

What did the mummy say to the tomb robber when he strangled him?

"The *choke's* on you."

What was the speed limit in Egypt?

70 *Nile*s an hour.

How did the mummy unravel?

He stepped on a wad of chewing gum
and kept on walking.

What did female mummies use on their faces instead of lipstick?

Glue stick.

Why was the mummy so grouchy in the morning?

He got up on the wrong side of the coffin.

Why don't mummies have any time to relax?

They're extremely *B.C.*

What did they call it when a pyramid came crashing to the ground?

A blast from the past.

What is the creepiest part of saying good morning to a mummy?

Watching him crawl out of bed.

How did tomb spiders advertise?

On their *web*site.

How was the hungry mummy's appetite?

*Fear*ocious.

What did mummies call a popular old-time song?

A golden *moldy*.

What event did the mummy win at the Olympic Games?

The 100 meter stagger.

What did mummies use to keep the wrappings from falling off their hands?

Thumbtacks.

Where did mummies look up old phone numbers?

In the *yellowed* pages.

What happened to the explorer who found the tomb of the pharaoh's barber?

He had a close shave.

Why did the Egyptian queen change her will?

She was having a bad *heir* day.

Where do you bury half a mummy?

In a *semi*tery.

What made the mummy's party so expensive?

Buying 3,000 candles for the birthday cake.

"Knock! Knock!"

"Who's there?"

"C.D."

"C.D. who?"

"C.D. man on de camel?"

Why did the mummy climb up the palm tree on Saturday night?

He wanted to get a date.

Why did the funeral director bury the corpse by the Nile?

He wanted to keep his *mummy* in the bank.

Why did the mummy donate his body to science?

He heard it was all for a good *gauze*.

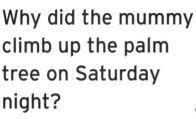

Why did the mummy complain?

He had a bone to pick.

When did the mummy get off his chariot?

When it came to a dead stop.

Where did the king park his camel?

In the *camel-lot*.

How was the charming mummy like a banana?

She was a-*peel*-ing.

How do you find the entrance to a tomb?

Just make a *fright* turn.

Why did the queen mummy wrap herself in dough?

She wanted to be a *roll* model.

Why did the scribe swing a papyrus scroll at the two vultures?

He wanted to kill two birds with one *tome*.

Why did the worried mummy push open the lid of his coffin?

He had to get it off his chest.

When visitors to the tomb saw a dog's ghost, what kind of dog did they see?

A French *boo!*-dle.

Joe: How can we ever outrun that mummy?
Anna: We don't have to. All *I* have to do is outrun *you!*

Glossary

Alexander the Great: A brave Macedonian king who liberated Egypt from the Persians.

Amulet (AM-yu-let): An ancient Egyptian good-luck charm.

Amun (AH-mun) or **Amen** (AH-men): The chief god of the Egyptian nation.

Ankh: The Egyptian symbol for "life."

Anubis (a-NEW-bis): Egyptian god of funerals.

Cairo (KAI-row): The modern capital of Egypt.

Cheops (KEY-ops): The pharaoh who built the Great Pyramid.

Cleopatra (klee-o-PAT-trah): A queen who ruled over Egypt in the days of ancient Rome.

Copts: Early Christians who lived in Egypt.

Hieroglyphics (high-eh-row-GLIF-ics): Egyptian writing that used pictures instead of letters.

Horus (HOR-us): The divine son of Osiris, god of the afterlife.

Isis (EYE-sis): The divine wife of Osiris.

Julius Caesar (JOO-lee-us SEE-zar): A dictator of Rome who loved Cleopatra.

King Tutankhamun (TOOT-ank-AH-mun): The teenaged king whose tomb was found filled with gold.

Mark Antony (AN-toe-nee): A brave Roman soldier who fell in love with Cleopatra.

Mesopotamia (MESS-o-po-TAY-mi-ah): The ancient name for the land of Iraq.

Nile: Egypt's great river.

Papyrus (pa-PIE-rus): The paper Egyptians wrote on.

Pepi (PEH-pee): A king who ruled Egypt at the end of the Pyramid Age.

Pharaoh (FAIR-oh): The title given to Egyptian rulers.

Pyramid (PEER-a-mid): A monumental tomb for Egyptian rulers.

Ra (RAH or RAY): The Egyptian god of the sun.

Rosetta (row-ZEH-tah) **Stone:** An inscribed stone that became the key to deciphering hieroglyphics.

Sahara (sah-HAH-rah): The world's largest hot desert, located in Northern Africa.

Sarcophagus (sar-KAH-fah-gus): A stone box that held a coffin.

Scribe: A writer who wrote and copied documents.

Sphinx (SFINKS): A huge statue in the Egyptian desert shaped like a reclining lion with a man's head.

Thebes (THEEBS): The capital of Egypt in the days of its Empire.

Tut: See "King Tutankhamun" on the previous page.

Some Children's Books about Ancient Egypt

Aliki. *Mummies: Made in Egypt*. New York: HarperCollins, 1985.

David, Rosalie. *Growing Up in Ancient Egypt*. New York: Troll Communications, 1997.

Green, John, and Stanley Appelbaum. *Life in Ancient Egypt Coloring Book*. New York: Dover Publications, 1989.

Harris, Geraldine, and Delia Pemberton. *Illustrated Encyclopedia of Ancient Egypt*. New York: Peter Bedrick, 2001.

Hart, Avery, Paul Mantell, and Michael Kline. *Pyramids: 50 Hands-On Activities to Experience Ancient Egypt*. Nashville, Tenn.: Williamson Publishing Company, 1997.

Hart, George. *Ancient Egypt*. New York: DK Children, 2008.

Honan, Linda. *Spend the Day in Ancient Egypt: Projects and Activities That Bring the Past to Life*. New York: Wiley, 1999.

Lester, Julius. *Pharaoh's Daughter: A Novel of Ancient Egypt*. New York: HarperTrophy, 2000.

Mayer, Josephine. *Never to Die: The Egyptians in Their Own Words*. Whitefish, Mont.: Kessinger Publishing, 2005 (1938).

Payne, Elizabeth. *The Pharaohs of Ancient Egypt*. New York: Random House, 1964.

Schlein, Miriam and Erik Hilgerdt. *I, Tut: The Boy Who Became Pharaoh*. New York: Four Winds, 1979.

Winters, Kay. *Voices of Ancient Egypt*. Washington, D.C.: National Geographic Children's Books, 2009.

About the Author

STEVE BERTMAN first became fascinated with archaeology when he was in fourth grade. After studying Latin in high school, he attended New York, Brandeis, and Columbia Universities, where he obtained degrees in Classics and Near Eastern Studies.

Steve is now Professor Emeritus of Classical Studies at Canada's University of Windsor, where he taught a very popular course entitled "Land of the Pharaohs" for many years. He is also the author of many serious books, including *Handbook to Life in Ancient Mesopotamia* (Oxford University Press) and *The Eight Pillars of Greek Wisdom* (Barnes & Noble). Though many editors and critics have laughed at his writings in the past, *Funny Mummy* is Steve Bertman's first deliberately humorous book.

Steve lives in West Bloomfield, Michigan, with his wife, Elaine. Their two children, Laura and Matthew, and their five grandchildren, Andrew, Josh, Jordyn, Logan, and Brandon, live nearby. It was for them and *their* children that this book was originally written.